# Solo

# repertoire

## FOR THE YOUNG PIANIST

T0081437

Compiled and Edited by
# William Gillock

ISBN 978-1-5400-7153-8

**WILLIS MUSIC**

EXCLUSIVELY DISTRIBUTED BY

**HAL•LEONARD®**

Visit Hal Leonard Online at
**www.halleonard.com**

Contact us:
**Hal Leonard**
7777 West Bluemound Road
Milwaukee, WI 53213
Email: info@halleonard.com

In Europe, contact:
**Hal Leonard Europe Limited**
42 Wigmore Street
Marylebone, London, W1U 2RN
Email: info@halleonardeurope.com

In Australia, contact:
**Hal Leonard Australia Pty. Ltd.**
4 Lentara Court
Cheltenham, Victoria, 3192 Australia
Email: info@halleonard.com.au

# Contents

# A Little Mazurka

John Thompson

# Choral Prelude

Felix Le Couppey

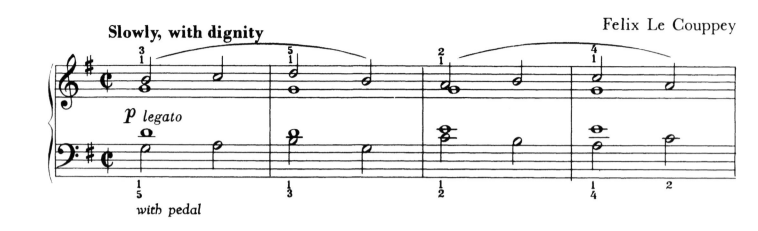

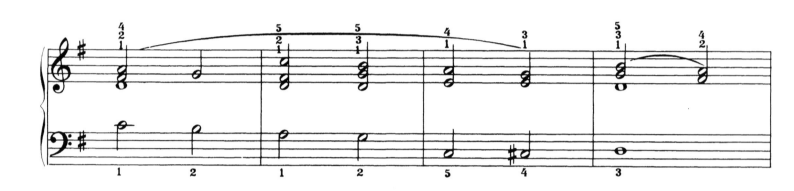

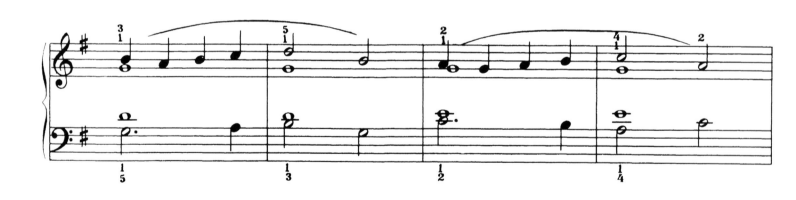

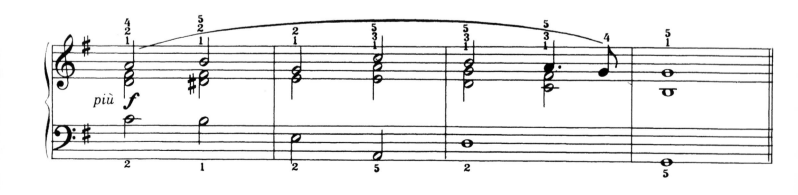

# Minuet

George Phillip Telemann

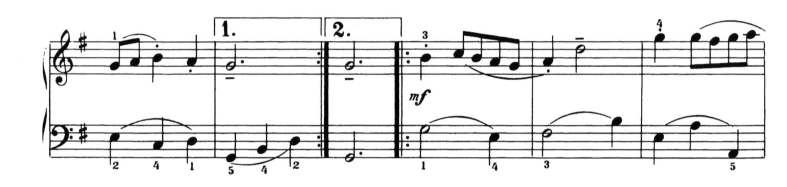

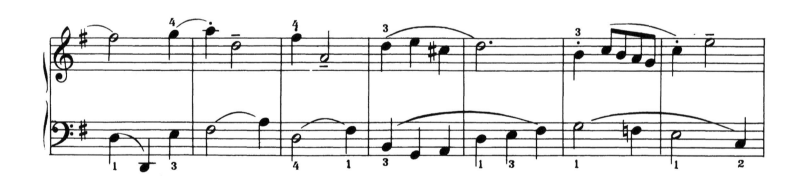

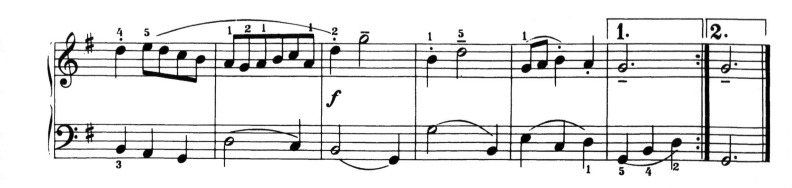

# After The Ball

Alexander Gretchaninoff

**In mazurka style**

# Festive Dance

Cornelius Gurlitt

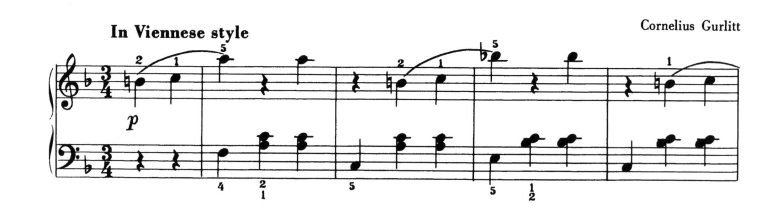

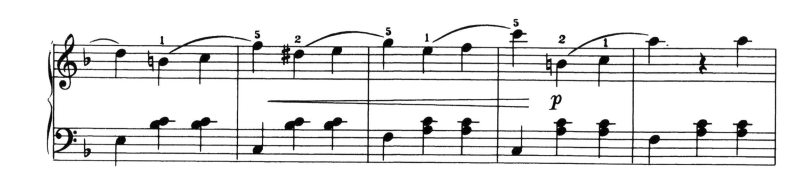

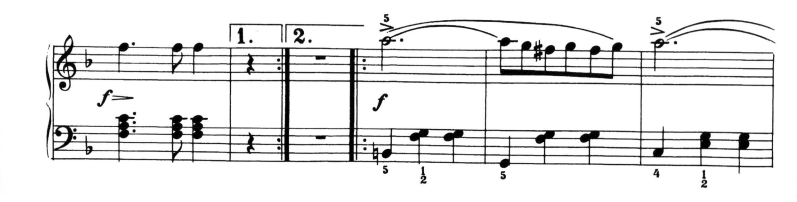

# A Dance At Versailles

John Thompson

**In minuet style - not fast**

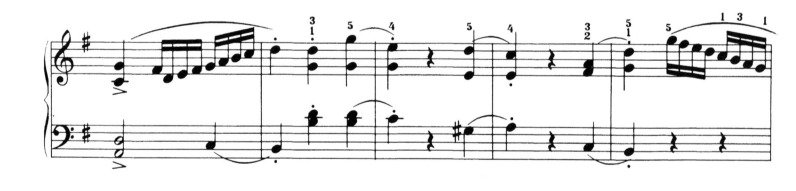

# Fife And Drum

Olive Russell

fading away

# Bells Of Notre Dame

Felix Le Couppey

**Smoothly**

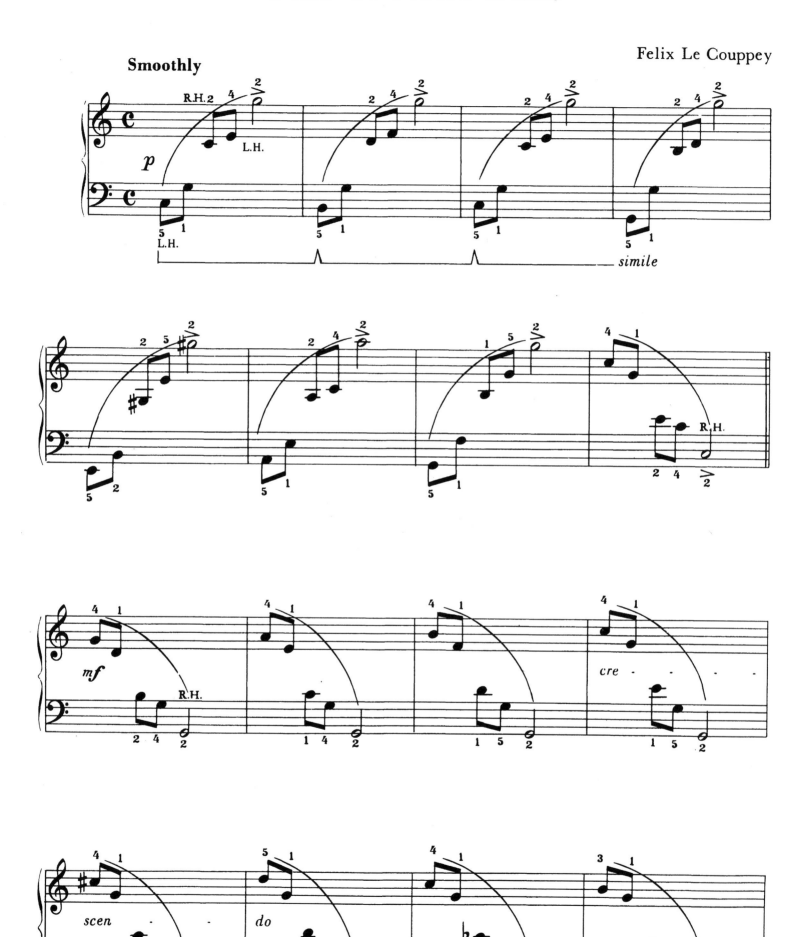

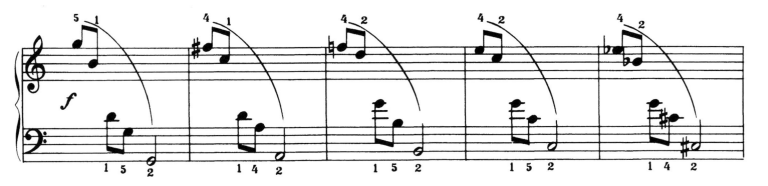

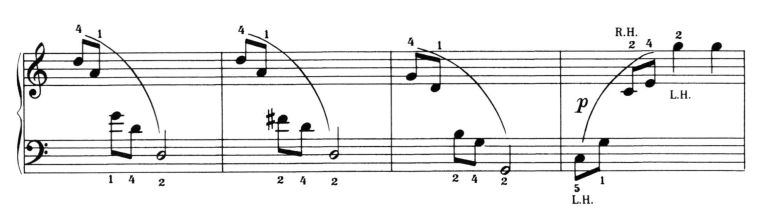

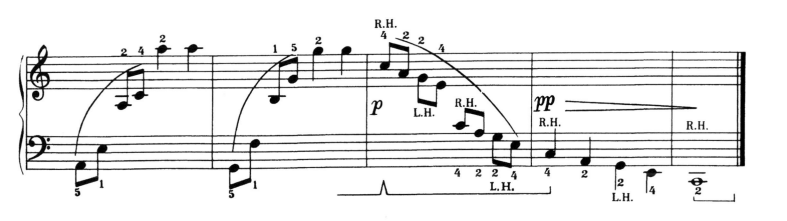

# The Fifers

Jean-François Dandrieu

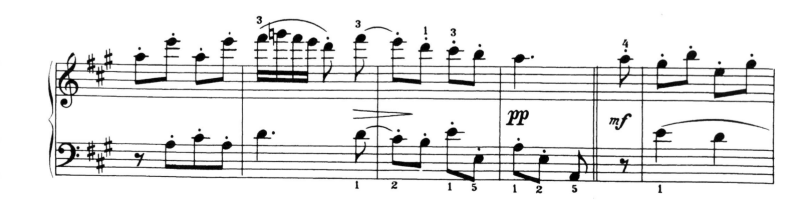

# The Seven Dwarfs

Alexander Gretchaninoff

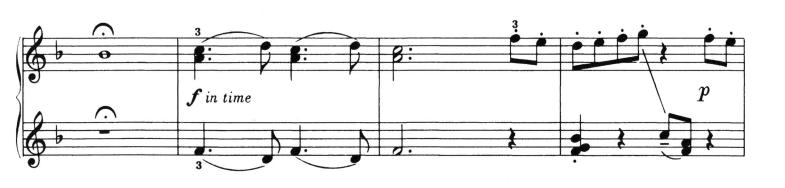

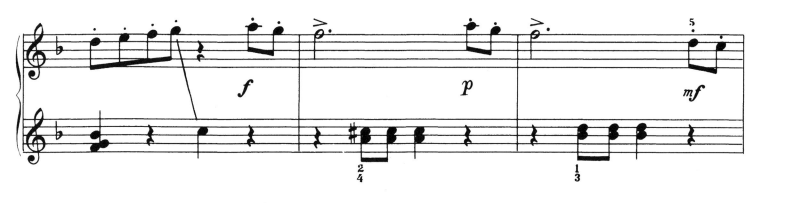

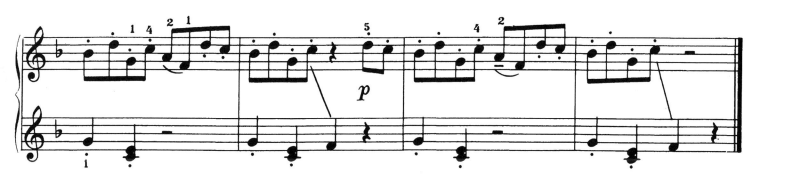

# Folk Song

Béla Bartók

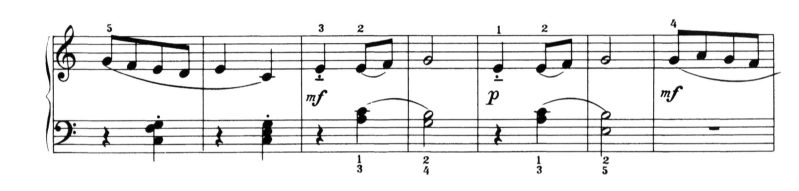

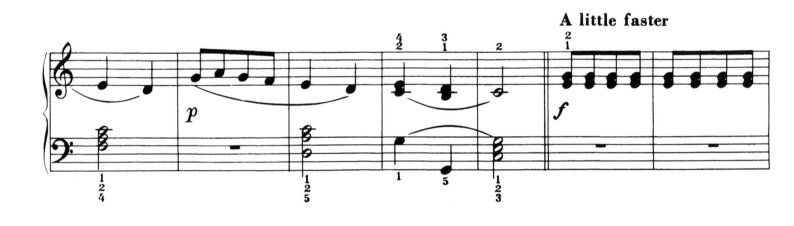

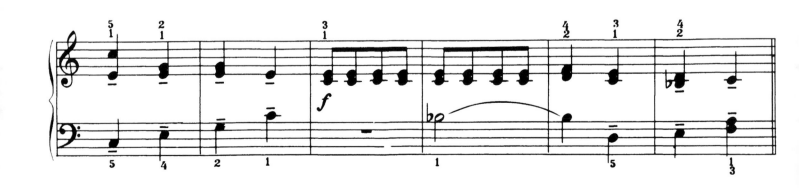

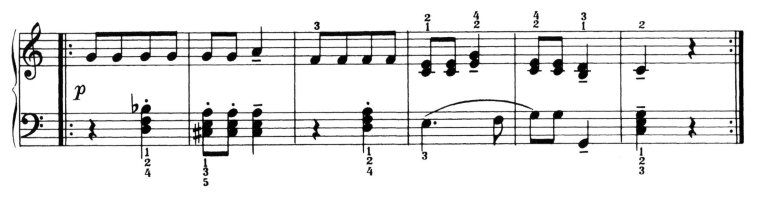

**Tempo I**

# Hopping

Dmitri Kabalevsky

**Energetically**

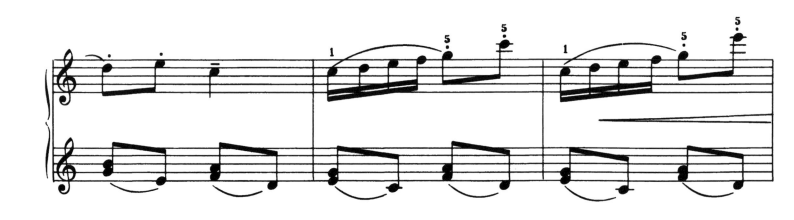

# The Sick Doll

Peter Illyitch Tchaikovsky

**With slow movement, expressively**

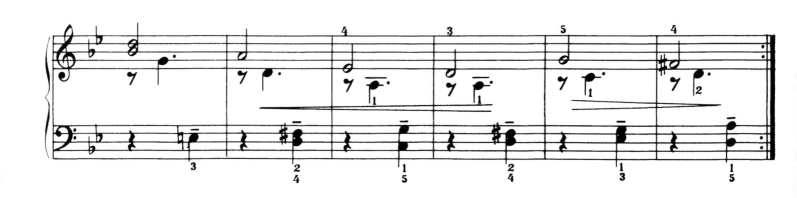

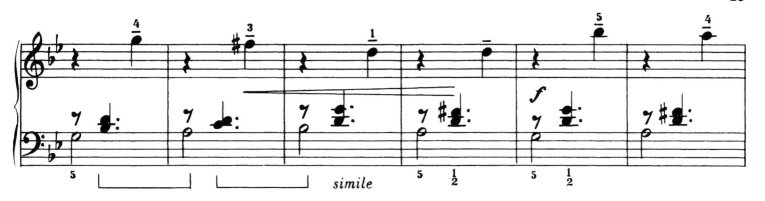

*simile*

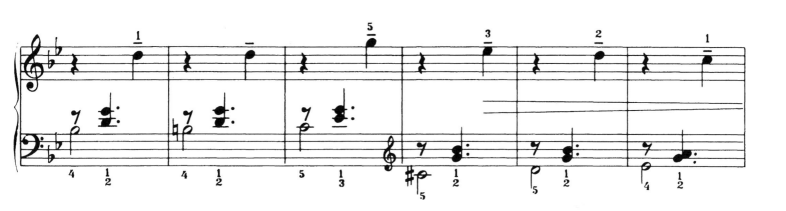

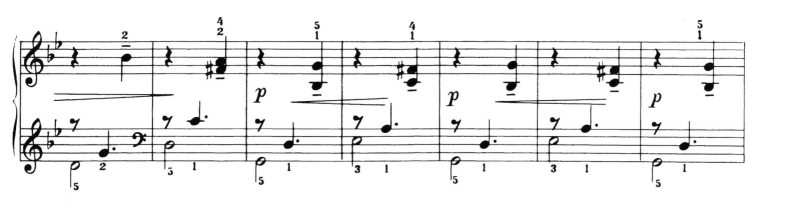

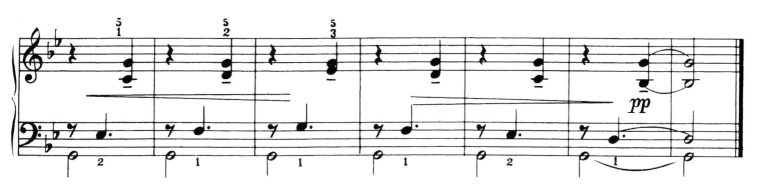

# The Wood Thrush

Irene Rodgers

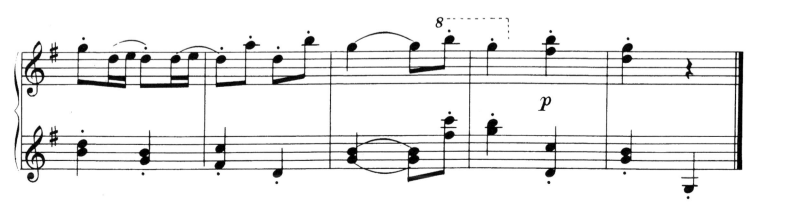

# Old French Song

Peter Illyitch Tchaikovsky

**Slowly - rather sadly**

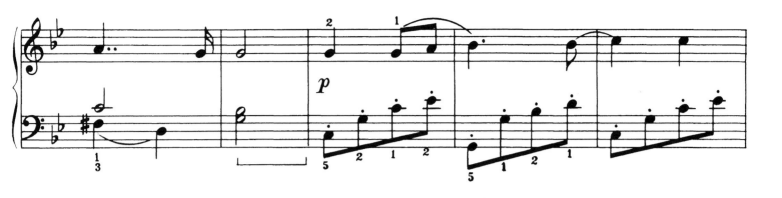

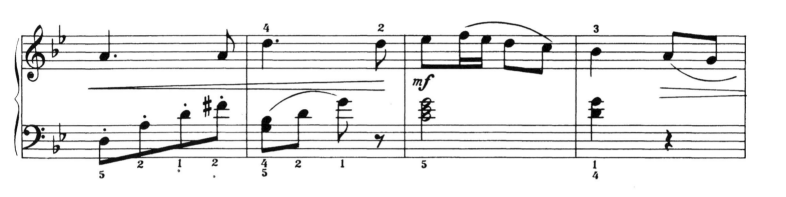

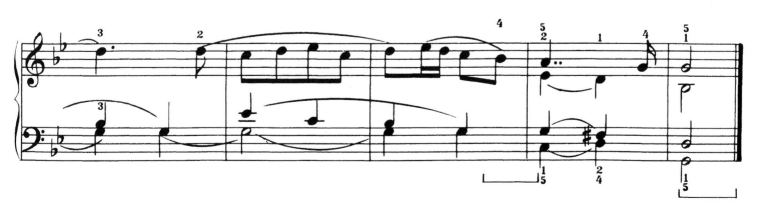

# Dance

Béla Bartók

# Arietta

Hugo Reinhold

# Sonatina

T. Salutrinskaya